A NAVPR----

MW01088095

*A life-changing
encounter with God's Word*

JESUS'
PASSION WEEK

*Our Savior's final days on earth
show us His love, character, and mission*

*A NavPress resource published in alliance
with Tyndale House Publishers*

NavPress.com

Written by Joyce Koo Dalrymple

The Team:
David Zimmerman, Publisher; Caitlyn Carlson, Acquisitions Editor; Elizabeth Schroll, Copyeditor; Olivia Eldredge, Operations Manager; Sarah Susan Richardson, Designer

Cover photograph of linen fabric by Luca Laurence on Unsplash.com.

Cover photograph of fabric texture copyright © Rawpixel. All rights reserved.

Author photo by Stephen Hong, copyright © 2019. All rights reserved.

For information about special discounts for bulk purchases, please contact Tyndale House Publishers at csresponse@tyndale.com, or call 1-855-277-9400.

ISBN 978-1-64158-821-8

Printed in the United States of America

30	29	28	27	26	25	24
7	6	5	4	3	2	1

CONTENTS

HOW TO USE THIS STUDY

Objectives

The topical guides in the LifeChange series of Bible studies cover important topics from the Bible. Although the LifeChange guides vary with the topics they explore, they share some common goals:

1. to help readers grasp what key passages in the Bible say about the topic;

2. to provide readers with explanatory notes, word definitions, historical background, and cross-references so that the only other reference they need is the Bible;

3. to teach readers how to let God's Word transform them into Christ's image;

4. to provide small groups with a tool that will enhance group discussion of each passage and topic; and

5. to write each session so that advance preparation for group members is strongly encouraged but not required.

Each lesson in this study is designed to take forty-five minutes to complete.

Overview and Details

The study begins with an overview of Jesus' Passion Week and journey to the Cross. The key to interpretation for each part of this study is content (what is the referenced passage *about*?), and the key to context is purpose (what is the author's *aim* for the passage as it relates to the overall topic?). Each lesson of the study explores the story from Jesus' final week on earth with a corresponding passage from the Bible.

Kinds of Questions

Bible study provides different lenses and perspectives through which to engage the Scripture: observe (what does the passage *say*?), interpret (what does the passage *mean*?), and apply (how does this truth *affect* my life?). Some of the "how" and "why" questions will take some creative thinking, even prayer, to answer. Some are opinion questions without clear-cut right answers; these will lend themselves to discussions and side studies.

Don't let your study become an exercise in knowledge alone. Treat the passage as God's Word, and stay in dialogue with Him as you study. Pray, *Lord, what do You want me to see here?*, *Father, why is this true?*, and *Lord, how does this apply to my life?*

It is important that you write down your answers. The act of writing clarifies your thinking and helps you to remember what you're learning.

Study Aids

Throughout the guide, there are study aids that provide background information on the passage, insights from commentaries, and word studies. These aids are included in the guide to help you interpret the Bible without needing to use other, outside resources. Still, if you're interested in exploring further, the full resources are listed in the endnotes.

Scripture Versions

Unless otherwise indicated, the Bible quotations in this guide are from the New International Version of the Bible. The other versions cited are the English Standard Version and the New Living Translation.

Use any translation you like for study—or preferably more than one. Ideally you would have on hand a good, modern translation such as the New International Version, the English Standard Version, the New Living Translation, or the Christian Standard Bible. A paraphrase such as *The Message* is not accurate enough for study, but it can be helpful for comparison or devotional reading.

Memorizing and Meditating

A psalmist wrote, "I have hidden your word in my heart that I might not sin against you" (Psalm 119:11). If you write down a verse or passage that challenges or encourages you and reflect on it often for a week or more, you will find it beginning to affect your motives and actions. We forget quickly what we read once; we remember what we ponder.

When you find a significant verse or passage, you might copy it onto a card to keep with you. Set aside five minutes each day just to think about what the passage might mean in your life. Recite it to yourself, exploring its meaning. Then, return to the passage as often as you can during the day for a brief review. You will soon find it coming to mind spontaneously.

For Group Study

A group of four to ten people allows for the richest discussions, but you can adapt this guide for other-sized groups. It will suit a wide range of group types, such as home Bible studies, growth groups, youth groups, and workplace Bible studies. Both new and experienced Bible students, and new and mature Christians, will benefit from the guide. You can omit or leave for later any questions you find too easy or too hard.

The guide is intended to lead a group through one lesson per meeting. This guide is formatted so you will be able to discuss each of the questions at length. Be sure to make time at each discussion for members to ask about anything they didn't understand.

Each member should prepare for a meeting by writing answers for all the background and discussion questions to be covered. Application will be very difficult, however, without private thought and prayer.

Two reasons for studying in a group are accountability and support. When each member commits in front of the rest to seek growth in an area of life, you can pray for one another, listen jointly for God's guidance, help one another resist temptation, assure each other that each person's growth matters to you, use the group to practice spiritual principles, and so on. Pray about one another's commitments and needs at most meetings. If you wish, you can spend the first few minutes of each meeting sharing any results from applications prompted by previous lessons and discuss new applications toward the end of the meeting. Follow your time of sharing with prayer for these and other needs.

If you write down what others have shared, you are more likely to remember to pray for them during the week, ask about what they shared at the next meeting, and notice answered prayers. You might want to get a notebook for prayer requests and discussion notes.

Taking notes during discussion will help you remember to follow up on ideas, stay on the subject, and have clarity on an issue. But don't let note-taking keep you from participating.

Some best practices for groups:

1. If possible, come to the group discussion prepared. The more each group member knows about the passage and the questions being asked, the better your discussion will be.

2. Realize that the group leader will not be teaching from the passage but instead will be facilitating your discussion. Therefore, it is important for each group member to participate so that everyone can contribute to what you learn as a group.

3. Try to stick to the passage covered in the session and the specific questions in the study guide.

4. Listen attentively to the other members of the group when they are sharing their thoughts about the passage. Also realize that most of the questions are open-ended, allowing for more than one answer.

5. Be careful not to dominate the discussion—especially if you are the leader. Allow time for everyone to share their thoughts and ideas.

6. As mentioned previously, throughout the session are study aids that provide background information on the passage, insights from commentaries, and word studies. Reading these aloud during the meeting is optional and up to the discussion leader. However, each member can refer to these insights if they found them helpful in understanding the passage.

A Note on Topical Studies

LifeChange guides offer robust and thoughtful engagement with God's Word. The book-centric guides focus on a step-by-step walk through that particular book of the Bible. The topical studies use Scripture to help you engage more deeply with God's Word and its implications for your life.

JESUS' PASSION WEEK

IF YOU KNEW YOU ONLY HAD ONE WEEK LEFT TO LIVE, what would you do? Who would you see, and what would you say to them?

Jesus' last week on earth is called the Passion Week. *Passio* is a Latin rendering of the Greek word *pathos*. The word connotes suffering, deep emotion, and longing.[1] Our final words and actions reveal what we are truly passionate about and what kind of legacy we want to leave. In this LifeChange study guide, we'll look closely at Jesus' last week leading up to the Crucifixion to understand the deep longings of His heart and the mission He came to accomplish.

The passionate love of God moved Jesus to enter the sufferings of humankind and endure the Cross. Both love and agony accompanied Jesus through each day of Passion Week.

- On Sunday, Jesus wept as He longed for His people to experience true peace and escape the consequences of Jerusalem's future destruction.

- On Monday, moved by holy anger, Jesus cleansed the Temple to remove obstacles that kept Gentiles and people experiencing poverty from being able to worship God.

- On Tuesday, in the face of great hostility, Jesus amazed the crowd by teaching with an authority that demonstrated His divine kingship.

- On Wednesday, Jesus graciously welcomed and received a woman who anointed Him in preparation for burial.

- On Thursday, Jesus demonstrated the full extent of His love to His disciples by washing their feet and giving them the gift of the Last Supper. Later that evening, His prayers at the garden of Gethsemane revealed His deep agony and submission to the Father's will.

- On Friday, Jesus performed the ultimate act of love by laying down His life on the cross to redeem the world.

Jesus' last days show that He was not just leaving behind a legacy; He was launching a new kingdom. This kingdom would be established not by force but by the power of His sacrificial love. Jesus was not the kind of king that people expected Him to be, motivated by power and nationalism. Rather, He ushered in a kingdom founded upon righteousness and justice, where the humble would be lifted up and the proud brought low. Jesus paid special attention to the oppressed, the excluded, and the people experiencing poverty because His Kingdom is one where all people are welcomed. Through His death and resurrection, He brought peace to those who are far away and peace to those who are near.

Jesus embodied the height and depth of God's love in a person, demonstrated by servanthood, suffering, and sacrifice. Ultimately, He made this love accessible to us through what He accomplished on the cross. Jesus invites us to receive His amazing love poured out for us in His life and death and to follow in His footsteps: "As I have loved you, so you must love one another. By this everyone will know that you are my disciples, if you love one another" (John 13:34-35). As you study Jesus' last week, may you be moved by the passion of Jesus, transformed by the power of the Holy Spirit, and inspired to lead a life of sacrificial love.

JESUS APPROACHES JERUSALEM

Luke 19:28-44

Palm Sunday

[Jesus said,] "If you, even you, had only known on this day what would bring you peace—but now it is hidden from your eyes."
LUKE 19:42

ON THE FIRST DAY OF PASSOVER, Jesus entered Jerusalem with a price upon His head—and He did so in a manner that publicly announced His kingship. Previously, He had avoided attracting the attention of the religious rulers, but now Jesus would make a final public appeal of love to the people to receive Him as their king.

As Jesus rode into Jerusalem on a donkey that had never been ridden, fulfilling an Old Testament prophecy (Zechariah 9:9), the crowd praised God: "Blessed is the king who comes in the name of the Lord! Peace in heaven and glory in the highest!" (Luke 19:38). But the people celebrating that day missed seeing who Jesus really is and what He came to do. Kings rode horses in wartime processions but donkeys in times of peace. The crowd expected Jesus to come as a conquering hero, freeing the Jews from the oppression of Rome, but Jesus was demonstrating that He came to His people in love and peace—to suffer and die for them.[1]

As He approached Jerusalem, Jesus saw the city across the Kidron Valley and wept (Luke 19:41). While the crowd shouted, "Hosanna!" Jesus sobbed—not for the suffering He was going to face that week but for His people and the destruction their rebellion would bring.[2]

"If you, even you, had only known on this day what would bring you peace," He said, "but now it is hidden from your eyes" (Luke 19:42). How He yearned for

1

them to know Him as the long-awaited Messiah whose Kingdom would have no end and who could bring them true *shalom* (the Hebrew word for peace, health, and wholeness). Jesus' reign would extend not only to Israel but to the ends of the earth, bringing peace to all the nations (Zechariah 9:10). As one commentary notes, "'This day' . . . of peace has arrived; and the city . . ., whose very name means 'peace,' has failed to recognize it."[3] At the very hour of His triumphal entry into Jerusalem, Jesus' heart overflowed with sorrowful longing for His people.

According to Porterfield, this vision of peace, in which everything is as it ought to be, touches every aspect of life and can never coexist with injustice. This is the kind of peace that Jesus, the Prince of Peace, came to bring.[5]

1. Author Jason Porterfield says, "Shalom exists when all our relationships are flourishing: our relationship with God, with each other, with creation, and even with ourselves."[4] In what areas of your life are you longing for shalom?

_____

_____

_____

_____

_____

_____

_____

2. Read Luke 19:28-40. What stands out to you about this passage?

_____

_____

_____

_____

_____

_____

_____

3. What phrases and images in this passage point to Jesus' kingship?

_____

_____

_____

_____

_____

_____

_____

_____

_____

_____

_____

4. What phrases and images in this passage point to Jesus' humble circumstances? How is Jesus different from the kind of king the people may have expected?

_____

_____

_____

_____

_____

_____

_____

_____

_____

_____

_____

The crowd enthusiastically threw their cloaks on the road, which was the customary way to coronate a new king (Luke 19:35-37; see also 2 Kings 9:13). They waved palm-tree branches and shouted "Hosanna!" (Matthew 21:9; Mark 11:9; John 12:13), which not only carried a sense of adoration but also reflected their belief that Jesus was coming to their rescue. Palm branches were a symbol of Israel's quest for independence from the time of the Maccabean revolt, an attempt to recapture Jerusalem from the Seleucid Empire (around 167 BC).[6]

New Testament scholar and pastor Michael Chung writes, "Jesus's coming offered the nation great hope that a king as great as David would lead the military of Israel over Roman rule.... He will fulfill the covenant God made with David in 2 Sam 7:11-16 where someone from the house of David will sit on the throne of Israel forever.... When the Jews see Jesus on the colt, they will associate Jesus as the Davidic king they have been expecting for over six hundred years."[7]

Jesus rode on a borrowed donkey; His disciples' cloaks served as His saddle; and the cloaks people threw down were probably inexpensive garments, tattered shawls, and dusty rags.[8] "The king of sinners and outcasts, the poor and the oppressed, calls us to join the worship of the one who 'has brought down the powerful from their thrones, / and lifted up the lowly ... filled the hungry with good things, / and sent the rich away empty' ([Luke] 1:52-53)."[9]

Theologian and scholar N. T. Wright writes how we have misunderstood the Gospels: "Most Christians, certainly in the Western churches, still assume that the whole purpose of the Christian faith is so that we might 'go to heaven when we die.'"[10] But Wright asserts that through Jesus, God launched a "new world, God's 'kingdom' of powerful creative and restorative love, arriving 'on earth as it is in heaven.'"[11] It is within this kingdom that a "new way of life was not only possible, but mandatory for Jesus's followers . . . Jesus's followers now have a mission."[12]

5. Does viewing Jesus as the King who came to usher in the Kingdom of God, and not only as your personal Savior who came to forgive your sins, change how you understand the gospel? If so, how?

_____
_____
_____
_____
_____
_____
_____
_____
_____

6. Jesus was not excited by the crowd's applause or shouts of praise. He was looking for true disciples whose hearts were turned toward Him and who would be committed to following Him. What is the difference between praising God with our lips and making Jesus King and Lord of our lives? What does that shift require?

_____
_____
_____
_____
_____
_____
_____
_____
_____
_____

7. Read Luke 19:41-44. At the same hour that Jesus was being hailed as king, He was overcome by sorrow. Why do you think Jesus wept?

The Greek verb used in verse 41 *(klaiō)* suggests that rather than shedding a few tears, Jesus audibly sobbed.[13]

_____

_____

_____

_____

_____

_____

_____

_____

_____

_____

8. We first see Jesus express His sorrow and longing for Jerusalem earlier in the book of Luke. In that instance, He also prophetically predicted its desolation (Luke 13:34-35). What metaphor did Jesus use to express His longing for Jerusalem (also in Matthew 23:37-38)? What does this communicate about the kind of relationship God desires to have with us?

Anglican priest and author Tish Harrison Warren observes, "Here he weeps not in rage at death, but in the sorrow of unrequited love. It's a deeply maternal image: Jesus longs to gather up children, wrap them up in the safety and intimacy of his embrace. But they refuse. . . . Any mother who has had to sit and watch her child destroy himself . . . knows something about how Jesus wept over Jerusalem."[14]

_____

_____

_____

_____

_____

_____

_____

_____

_____

We relate to God in our pain through lament. Over one-third of the Psalms contain prayers of lament. Pastor Mark Vroegop writes, "Lament is the honest cry of a hurting heart wrestling with the paradox of pain and the promise of God's goodness."[15]

9. Living in the brokenness of this world, we may long for things that are not yet fulfilled. Jesus' lament gives us permission to express our grief more openly to God. What everyday sufferings or particular hardships in your own life do you need to grieve? Are there any spiritual practices that can help you express your lament to God?

_____

_____

_____

_____

_____

_____

_____

_____

Your Response

How do you think Jesus feels today when He looks at the earth? Ask Jesus to make our hearts like His, that we may notice and deeply care about the things He cares about. Share one thing that God has given you a passion for or drawn your attention to that reflects His heart. How can you use your gifts in that area?

_____

_____

_____

_____

_____

_____

_____

_____

For Further Study

Read Exodus 12:1-6. Jesus rode into Jerusalem on the one day each year that Jewish shepherds herded huge flocks of Passover lambs into Jerusalem for worshipers to select. The first day of Passover coincided with the tenth day of the Jewish month of Nisan. On that day, each family was to select a one-year-old male lamb without blemish. According to Jewish historians, the sheep were brought from Bethlehem to Jerusalem. Four days later, the community of Israel would slaughter their lambs, giving each household time to check that their lamb was without any defect.[16] What parallels do you notice between Jesus' journey to the Cross and the way the lambs were chosen and sacrificed in the Old Testament? What is the significance of Jesus being called the Lamb of God (John 1:29)?

JESUS CLEANSES THE TEMPLE

Matthew 21:12-22

Holy Monday

[Jesus said,] "'My house will be called a house of prayer,' but you are making it 'a den of robbers.'"
MATTHEW 21:13

DURING THE PASSOVER, people traveled to Jerusalem from all over Israel to offer sacrifices at the Temple. The Temple in Jerusalem represented the dwelling place of God on earth: a place of holiness where the Presence of God lived among His people. God intended it to be a place where all could come, so it angered the heart of God when certain obstacles made it harder for some people to worship. The whole sacrificial system rested on the buying and selling of animals, and that practice had become mercenary, profiting some and marginalizing others.

On Monday, Jesus, the Holy One incarnate, entered the Temple to demonstrate holy anger at how His house was being defiled. Jesus overturned the tables of the money changers and the benches of those selling doves. "'My house will be called a house of prayer,' but you are making it 'a den of robbers'" (Matthew 21:13), Jesus said, quoting from the prophet Jeremiah, who also confronted the Israelites for making the Temple a "den of robbers" (Jeremiah 7:11).

Jesus' desire was for the Temple to be a house of prayer for all, including those on the margins. The people in charge used their power for their own benefit instead of for the benefit of those Jesus was trying to gather into His house. In overturning the tables and driving out the profiteers, Jesus wielded a righteous anger to powerfully demonstrate His loving protection of foreigners and people experiencing poverty. He also welcomed children and healed people who were physically disabled, those who were historically excluded from worshiping in the Temple. Lastly, Jesus cursed a fig tree for not bearing fruit (Matthew 21:19). God is not interested in a form of piety that neglects the vulnerable. He is looking for an authentic faith that expresses itself in love for others.

---

1. Read Matthew 21:12-17. What groups of people are present in this Temple scene? What is each group doing?

_____

_____

_____

_____

_____

_____

_____

The issue is less about the commerce itself than where the exchange takes place and potentially how its purpose became more about profit than worship. Purity laws excluded women and Gentiles from the Court of Israel. The money changers set up shop in the only part of the Temple where these populations were permitted, thus disrupting their ability to pray and worship.[1] These money changers and animal sellers also may have reaped a hefty profit at the expense of those coming to worship in the Temple, a practice that threatened to exclude people experiencing poverty.

2. Read Isaiah 56:6-7; Psalm 140:12; and Proverbs 17:5. What do these verses suggest about why Jesus was so angry at the money changers and animal sellers in Matthew 21:12-13?

_____

_____

_____

_____

_____

_____

_____

_____

3. Jesus demonstrated that anger can be a holy response to injustice, abuse, or oppression of the vulnerable. How can we use holy anger constructively to usher in the Kingdom of God?

_____

_____

_____

_____

_____

_____

_____

_____

_____

_____

_____

Pastor and author Rich Villodas says, "Throughout Holy Scripture, whenever there is abuse or neglect, God calls for a practical restructuring of concern, as well as the judgment of those in power. . . . Mercy means bandaging up people bloodied in life. Justice refers to systemically stopping those who are bloodying up people in the first place, and creating an environment for everyone's flourishing. Christ's followers are called to both kinds of ministries, especially on behalf of the poor and powerless."[2]

4. After Jesus drove out the money changers and animal sellers, what group of people came to Jesus for healing in verse 14? Why would this be countercultural for the Jewish leaders?

_____

_____

_____

_____

_____

_____

_____

_____

_____

"Mosaic law prohibited those with physical defects from offering sacrifices (Leviticus 21:16-24), and David had banned them from ever entering the temple (2 Samuel 5:8)."[3] Touching someone who was considered "unclean" would prevent a person from offering sacrifices at the Temple. Instead of becoming contaminated, Jesus healed and made clean those who encountered Him. "These two actions—cleansing the temple and the healing miracles—jointly declare his superiority over the temple."[4]

5. The children at the Temple praised Jesus, echoing what the crowd shouted during His triumphal entry: "Hosanna to the Son of David!" The religious leaders were unhappy with the children's shouts and with what Jesus was doing in the Temple. How does Jesus' response to the chief priests' question in verse 16 further reveal His identity as the Messiah?

_____

_____

_____

_____

_____

_____

_____

_____

_____

_____

Fig trees bear fruit close to when or shortly after their leaves emerge. Thus, regardless of whether figs were in season, this tree's leaves advertised that it should be bearing fruit. However, Jesus found no fruit on the tree; the advertisement was false. Jesus cursed the tree not because it was not bearing fruit but because it made a show of bearing fruit while remaining fruitless.[5]

6. Read Matthew 21:18-22. Why do you think Jesus cursed the fig tree?

_____

_____

_____

_____

_____

_____

_____

_____

_____

_____

7. How would you describe the connection between Jesus cursing the fig tree and Jesus cleansing the Temple?

_____

_____

_____

_____

_____

_____

_____

_____

_____

_____

_____

Jesus criticized the money changers and vendors (who were disrupting the ability of women and Gentiles to pray in the Temple) and the chief priests (who were indignant about the children's praises of the Messiah). He opposed those who put obstacles in the way of those who desired to worship Him. D. A. Carson explains: "These [people], like this leafy fig tree, Jesus finds full of advertised piety without any fruit—and them he curses."[6]

8. What can you infer from Matthew 21:12-22 about the kind of follower Jesus seeks? How is this different from what the religious leaders believed made a person "acceptable" before God?

_____

_____

_____

_____

_____

_____

_____

_____

_____

As author Alia Joy writes, Jesus was looking for those who are poor—not just materially, but poor in spirit: "His heart of compassion always bent toward those suffering under the burdens of injustice, poverty, and calamity. . . . Understanding Jesus's presence and incarnational approach to loving our neighbor will always have more to do with identification of our own areas of poverty than with a posture of thinking we're in any way the savior the poor need. The place of blessing we give from is our understanding that all is grace and everything belongs to God. . . . Grace levels us and humbles us to see our neighbor as ourselves."[7]

After Jesus' death and resurrection, Temple sacrifices would no longer be needed because Jesus provided the way to make us right with God. *All* people who put their faith in Christ have direct access to God through prayer.

9. The heart of the Temple was prayer, and sacrifice was a means to be made right with God and have access to Him. What did Jesus want the disciples to understand about prayer as they wondered at the withered fig tree in verses 20-22?

_____

_____

_____

_____

_____

_____

_____

_____

10. What is something you would like to bring to God in prayer that may feel like moving a mountain (verse 21)? Share your prayer request with others if you are comfortable doing so, and then pray about it together.

_____

_____

_____

_____

_____

_____

_____

_____

_____

Your Response

In this passage, Jesus condemned those who made a show of piety but took advantage of vulnerable people in His house. He welcomed those who came to Him in honesty and humility: those who desired healing, the little children who praised Him, and those who prayed with faith. How do you come to Jesus? What are some ways you can cultivate an authentic relationship with Jesus rather than just going through religious motions? Ponder how Jesus welcomes you with love and open arms.

For Further Study

In John 2, when the Jews asked Jesus for a sign to prove His authority to cleanse the Temple, Jesus replied, "Destroy this temple, and I will raise it again in three days" (John 2:19). Jesus was referring to His body as the Temple and pointing to His death and resurrection as the sign. N. T. Wright observes that "the Temple was the intersection between heaven and earth; but now the place of intersection is Jesus himself. . . . Heaven and earth are now joined in the person—in the risen body!—of Jesus himself. . . . The one who sits in heaven is the one who rules on earth."[8] In 1 Corinthians 3:16-17, the apostle Paul called all Jesus' followers God's temple because the Holy Spirit now dwells in us. We are now equipped with the Holy Spirit, individually and collectively, to be God's temple. How does viewing yourself and others as God's temple affect how you see yourself and treat other believers?

JESUS TEACHES AT THE TEMPLE

Mark 12:13-17

Holy Tuesday

[Jesus said,] "Give back to Caesar what is
Caesar's and to God what is God's."
MARK 12:17

JESUS' ACTIONS IN THE TEMPLE had created an uproar.
When Jesus returned to the Temple courts on Tuesday,
the chief priests, teachers of the law, and elders immediately approached Him to question His authority to
do such things (Mark 11:27-28). As the guardians of
the traditions of Israel and Temple practices, they felt
threatened. They wanted to arrest Him but were afraid
of the crowds (Matthew 21:46; Mark 12:12-13). So instead,
the Pharisees and Herodians sought to trap Him with
a series of questions that they hoped would turn the
people against Him.

The Pharisees saw Jesus as a threat to their religious authority. The Herodians, who supported the
pro-Roman Herodian dynasty, viewed Jesus as a
threat to Herodian rule. These two groups, which usu-
ally held opposing positions, banded together to trick
Jesus by posing this question: Should they pay taxes
to Caesar?

Jesus' answer was profound: "Give back to Caesar
what is Caesar's and to God what is God's" (Mark 12:17).
This raised a bigger question: What did those trying to
trap Him believe belongs to God? How they answered
that question would have ramifications for every part
of their lives, not just their taxes.

1. Describe a time when you or another Christian struggled with whether to obey an authority figure in your life because you believed doing so was contrary to God's will. What was your reaction to that experience? What did you observe about the reaction of others to that experience?

_____

_____

_____

_____

_____

_____

_____

_____

_____

_____

2. Read Mark 12:13-17. What stands out to you?

_____

_____

_____

_____

_____

_____

_____

_____

_____

_____

3. How was the question of whether to pay taxes to Caesar a trap?

_____
_____
_____
_____
_____
_____
_____
_____
_____
_____

If Jesus answered no, He would be guilty of treason against the state; the Herodians could arrest Him for being a threat to public order and hand Him to Roman authorities to be executed for sedition or treason.[1] But if He answered yes, the Pharisees would denounce Him as disloyal to Israel, thus alienating the crowd at the Temple. Many Jews considered the imposed Roman tax "an outrageous act of interference on the part of their foreign rulers."[2]

4. The tax was to be paid with a Roman denarius, which bore the head of the emperor with an inscription ("Tiberius Caesar, Son of the Divine Augustus") on one side and the image of the pagan goddess of peace on the other side.[3] Why would this coin be so offensive to pious Jews?

_____
_____
_____
_____
_____
_____
_____
_____
_____
_____

A Roman denarius violated both the first and second commandments: not to worship any other gods or to possess any graven images (Exodus 20:3-4; Deuteronomy 5:7-8).[4] Rome allowed Jews to make their own coins that didn't violate their commandments. It was more important to the empire that the taxes were paid, not how they were paid.[5] Thus, Jason Porterfield contends that when Jesus asked the Pharisees and Herodians for a denarius and they handed Him one, they unwittingly revealed that they not only possessed a denarius but had also brought one into the Temple.[6]

Porterfield asserts that the crowd would have realized Jesus was "alluding to the central Jewish tenet that all of humanity is created in God's *image*. The implication is this: Since the coin has Caesar's *image* imprinted on it, give it back to him. Let him keep his idolatrous money. But . . . since we have God's *image* imprinted on us, 'we owe everything—all that we have and all that we are—to him.'"[7] N. T. Wright similarly observes, "Perhaps it's time for God—whose image is on every human being and whose 'inscription' is written across the pages of creation and the story of Israel—to receive his due."[8]

5. In verse 14, the Pharisees and Herodians began by complimenting Jesus, saying, "You aren't swayed by others, because you pay no attention to who they are." The Greek (which here renders a Hebrew idiom) says literally, "You don't look at people's faces." But instead of repeating the word *face* in His reply, Jesus asked whose *image* was on the coin (verse 16). Read Genesis 1:27. What is significant about Jesus choosing to use the word *image*?

_____

_____

_____

_____

_____

_____

_____

_____

6. Jesus' answer—"Give back to Caesar what is Caesar's and to God what is God's"—begs the following question: What truly belongs to human authorities, and what belongs to God? How would you answer that question? Read Psalm 24:1; John 3:31; and Romans 13:1-8. How do those Scriptures inform your answer?

_____

_____

_____

_____

_____

_____

_____

_____

_____

7. Mark 12:17 has been interpreted to mean we are to give God our worship, but in all other things serve the governing earthly authorities. This has led people down a path of dualism, where God oversees spiritual matters but "Caesar" (governing authorities) is lord over all else.[9] Where do you see aspects of this dualism today? What are the consequences of this compartmentalization?

_____

_____

_____

_____

_____

_____

_____

8. As He sends His followers into a hostile world, Jesus knows they will encounter those who will try to tear them down. In Matthew 10:16, He tells His disciples to be "as shrewd as snakes and as innocent as doves." The disciples must be "shrewd as snakes" to avoid their traps. Yet they must also remain "innocent as doves," living a holy, blameless life. Considering these principles, how should we practically interact with people who may oppose us because of our work or faith in Christ? What can we learn from Jesus' example in Mark 12?

_____

_____

_____

_____

_____

_____

_____

_____

Your Response

Describe what it would look like to live as if everything belonged to God. How would that posture change your relationship with your money and possessions? How would that impact how you invest in meeting others' needs?

_____

_____

_____

_____

_____

_____

_____

_____

_____

_____

_____

_____

_____

_____

_____

_____

_____

_____

_____

_____

For Further Study

Read John 19:4-16. During Jesus' trial before Pilate, how did Jesus submit to what was happening to Him while also showing that He has ultimate authority? What did Jesus say was the source of Pilate's authority and power (verse 11)? Can you think of another example where human authority was tainted by evil but God still accomplished His redemptive purposes?

Session Four

JESUS IS ANOINTED AT BETHANY

Mark 14:1-10

Holy Wednesday

[Jesus said,] "She has done a beautiful thing to me. . . . She poured perfume on my body beforehand to prepare for my burial."

MARK 14:6, 8

WEDNESDAY WAS THE TURNING POINT.[1] Following Jesus' actions in the Temple, the chief priests and elders began plotting how to arrest and kill Jesus (Matthew 26:3-4; Mark 14:1-2). Later that day Judas Iscariot approached them to betray Jesus (Matthew 26:14-16; Mark 14:10-11). Amid this opposition, Simon threw a dinner party for Jesus and invited Martha, Mary, and Lazarus (John 12:1-3). Jesus, who was keenly aware of what lay ahead, welcomed this opportunity to be with a few of His closest friends and cherished the gift Mary of Bethany would give Him.

As He was reclining at the table, Mary boldly interrupted the gathering by breaking an alabaster jar of imported perfume, worth a year's wages, and pouring all of it over Jesus' head. Mary did not care that she was breaking social norms because her sole focus was on loving Jesus. While on the surface we might see what she did as a mere material offering, the implications are deeper: Mary's sacrifice was one of reverence, love, and worship. Her gift represented a giving of her whole self.

But the disciples could not see beyond the surface and harshly chastised Mary, calling what she did a "waste" (Matthew 26:8; Mark 14:4). They still did not understand that Jesus was headed to the Cross. Mary alone marked the significance of this moment with her lavish gift, in effect anointing Him for His burial. Jesus called what she did a "beautiful thing" and honored her by memorializing her act for posterity (Matthew 26:10, 13; Mark 14:6, 9). The scent of the perfume probably remained on Jesus' hair and skin for days. The fragrance of Mary's love and worship was something He must have treasured as He journeyed to the Cross.

1. Gifts are often an expression of love. In addition to the cost, the giver also invests time, thought, and effort in finding a special gift. Describe a meaningful gift you either gave or received. What did that gift indicate about the relationship between the giver and receiver?

_____

_____

_____

_____

_____

_____

_____

_____

_____

_____

_____

_____

_____

_____

_____

2. Read Mark 14:1-10. What events happen before (in verses 1-2) and after (in verses 10-11) the story of Jesus' anointing? What is the significance of His anointing happening between those two events?

_____

_____

_____

_____

_____

_____

_____

_____

_____

_____

_____

3. How do you think Jesus felt when He was in Bethany with His friends?

_____

_____

_____

_____

_____

_____

_____

_____

_____

_____

_____

Mary had a close relationship with Jesus that began when she sat at Jesus' feet to learn from Him (Luke 10:38-42). When Martha complained that Mary should be working with her instead, Jesus affirmed Mary's choice. When her brother Lazarus died, Mary fell at His feet, crying, "Lord, if you had been here, my brother would not have died" (John 11:32). Jesus wept with Mary and then raised her brother from the dead (John 11:33-43). Mary's love for Jesus grew through experiencing His compassionate love and life-saving power. This extravagant act of anointing expressed what Jesus meant to her. Perhaps she also grasped that Jesus' death was coming and that this might be one of the last times she would see Him.

4. John's Gospel identifies Mary of Bethany as the woman who anointed Jesus (John 12:3). She would have had to bring the alabaster jar of perfume from her own home to the house of Simon. Mary did not just spontaneously give Jesus the most valuable thing she had. She did this with great love and deliberation. Why do you think Mary decided to do this?

_____

_____

_____

_____

_____

_____

_____

_____

_____

Michael Chung writes, "While the anointing of Jesus's head points to royalty [marking Jesus's kingship], the anointing of his feet communicates Mary's worship and submission."[2]

5. In Mark's and Matthew's accounts of the event, Mary poured the perfume on Jesus' head (Matthew 26:6-7; Mark 14:3), and in John's account she poured the perfume on His feet and wiped His feet with her hair (John 12:3). What do you think is the significance of anointing someone's head versus someone's feet? Why are both appropriate ways to honor Jesus?

_____

_____

_____

_____

_____

_____

_____

_____

6. Immediately after this scene, Judas betrayed Jesus for thirty pieces of silver (Matthew 26:14-15; Mark 14:10). In Hebrew culture, thirty pieces of silver was not a lot of money. Thirty shekels (or about twelve ounces) of silver was the price paid to the master of a slave who was accidentally killed (Exodus 21:32). What do you think motivated Judas to betray Jesus?

By offering Judas thirty pieces of silver, the religious leaders were in effect equating Jesus' value with that of a dead slave.[3] If Judas was motivated solely by greed, he probably would have negotiated a higher price. Judas likely became Jesus' disciple in the first place because he wanted to take part in a political revolution to liberate Israel from its enemies. But as Jesus made known that He did not come to be a worldly, national king of the Jews, Judas realized that Jesus was not the kind of messiah he had signed up to follow.[4]

7. The perfume that Mary gave Jesus was her most valuable possession, probably a family heirloom.[5] The things that we value most are often what can hinder us from worshiping God with our whole heart. What do you value most? How can you cultivate a deeper love for and devotion toward Jesus, particularly in relation to what you value?

Theologian Craig S. Keener explains: "Sealing [the perfume] in such a container would preserve its fragrance, but once the bottle was broken, one would need to use up the perfume immediately."[6] The breaking of the alabaster jar symbolized the totality of Mary's gift.[7]

Jesus calls what Mary did a "beautiful" *(kalos)* thing. The Greek word *kalos* has an ethical or moral sense and can mean beautiful, good, or desirable. It can refer to something that is so attractively good that it inspires others to embrace what is beautiful and praiseworthy.[8]

8. Some of those present harshly rebuked Mary for what they considered a wasteful act (verse 4). They felt that they knew better than Mary and belittled her in front of Jesus. How surprised they must have been by Jesus' response! How does Jesus view Mary's gift? How does He honor her (verses 6-9)?

_____

_____

_____

_____

_____

_____

_____

_____

_____

_____

9. What do you think this experience with Mary meant to Jesus, especially in the days before His death?

_____

_____

_____

_____

_____

_____

_____

_____

_____

_____

Your Response

Mary broke with social norms to pour out her gift in an act of total love and worship. What are some tangible ways you are presently worshiping Jesus with how you spend your time, talent, or treasure? Think creatively about how you would like to do so in the future, even if it may mean breaking with convention.

For Further Study

In Luke 7:36-50, we read about another woman who poured perfume on Jesus' feet. Having lived a "sinful life," she understood how much Jesus had forgiven her, and in return, she expressed her great love for Jesus. She washed Jesus' feet with her tears, wiped them with her hair, and kissed them. How did the dinner host respond to this outpouring of devotion? How did Jesus commend this woman? What can we learn from both this woman's and Mary's example?

Session Five

JESUS WASHES THE DISCIPLES' FEET

John 13:1-20

Maundy Thursday

[Jesus said,] "A new command I give you: Love one another. As I have loved you, so you must love one another. By this everyone will know that you are my disciples, if you love one another."

JOHN 13:34-35

NOW THAT HIS TIME HAD COME to leave the world, Jesus focused on showing the disciples what He wanted them to remember: the full extent of His love. On their last evening together, Jesus broke social and cultural norms to show the disciples His love in a tangible way. Taking the role of a servant, Jesus stripped off His outer clothing and wrapped a towel around His waist. Then, stooping down, He tenderly washed and dried the disciples' feet. By serving in this way, Jesus foreshadowed the reason for His death: He was going to the Cross as the Suffering Servant who "did not come to be served, but to serve, and to give his life as a ransom for many" (Matthew 20:28).

Jesus wanted the disciples to receive His humble, self-giving love, but He didn't want that to be the end of it. They were to go and love others in the same way. He told them, "Now that I, your Lord and Teacher, have washed your feet, you also should wash one another's feet. I have set you an example that you should do as I have done for you" (John 13:14-15). This radical, action-oriented love would be how others would know that they were His disciples.

Ironically, the disciples had just been competing about who was the most important (Luke 22:24). In contrast to earthly kings, who may wield their power with a domineering authority, Jesus comes with a different kind of power (Luke 22:25-30). The reversal of social expectation reveals the true nature of God's Kingdom, where the last shall be first and the first shall be last (Matthew 19:30; 20:16). It is a Kingdom that is established not by force but by the "power of the servant" and by "the strength of love."[1]

1. What qualities do you look for in a leader? Why do you think people more often value eloquence or charisma in their leaders over humility and character? What would change in our workplaces, government institutions, and churches if the opposite were true?

_____

_____

_____

_____

_____

_____

_____

_____

_____

2. Read John 13:1-20. What stands out to you about Jesus in this story?

_____

_____

_____

_____

_____

_____

_____

_____

JESUS WASHES THE DISCIPLES' FEET

3. What do verses 1-3 and 18-19 reveal about what
Jesus knew? This knowledge shows that Jesus was
in control of the events leading up to His death.
With this in mind, what is the significance of
Jesus washing the disciples' feet at this time?

_____

_____

_____

_____

_____

_____

_____

_____

_____

4. Describe the kind of love Jesus demonstrated in
this passage.

_____

_____

_____

_____

_____

_____

_____

_____

_____

_____

_____

_____

In John 13:1, the verb *love*
occurs twice. In both cases,
the Greek word *agapaō*
is used. *Agapaō* refers to
deliberately choosing to
seek the good of the other.
Elsewhere John states, "God
is love" (1 John 4:8), using
the related noun *agapē*.
This kind of love is part of
God's character, and He is
its source. In sending Jesus
to die for us while we were
still sinners (Romans 5:8),
God set the standard for
agapē love. Biblical scholar
Robert Mounce observes
that in John 13:1, the Greek
expression *eis telos*, used
to describe Jesus' love, can
be translated two different
ways: Jesus loved them
"to the end" in a temporal
sense, or Jesus showed
them "the full extent" of His
love in a qualitative sense.
Mounce writes, "It is better
in this case not to separate
the two ideas, for because
the love of Jesus was of the
highest degree, it would
consequently carry through
to the very end."[2]

Mounce writes, "Peter's wholehearted commitment to his Master, along with his sense of the incongruity between lordship and humble service, . . . led him to react as he did. . . . Peter's intention was to prevent what he could not grasp, and in doing so revealed more pride than humility."[3] Sometimes it takes more humility to receive than to give. "The disciples' pride kept them from entering into a genuine understanding of and appreciation for the remarkable event they were privileged to witness."[4]

Professor Gail O'Day observed that "it is by accepting Jesus in the surprising role of loving host and intimate servant that one has a 'share' with him, that one receives the love of God incarnate. . . . The essence of the foot washing is Jesus' offer of himself in love. . . . The call for the disciples is to allow themselves to be ministered to in this way, to accept Jesus' gesture of love fully."[5]

5. Why do you think Peter was initially so adamant that Jesus not wash his feet (verses 6-8)?

6. What do you think Jesus meant when He said, "Unless I wash you, you have no part with me" (verse 8)?

7. In light of what Jesus was about to do on the cross for the disciples and all who would believe in Him, how do you understand Jesus' words in verse 10 that the disciples did not need a bath because their whole body was "clean"?

_____

_____

_____

_____

_____

_____

_____

_____

_____

_____

8. In John 13:34-35, Jesus says, "A new command I give you: Love one another. As I have loved you, so you must love one another. By this everyone will know that you are my disciples, if you love one another." Why do you think this is a new command?

_____

_____

_____

_____

_____

_____

_____

_____

_____

Pastor Derek Vreeland writes, "This was a new commandment, a new ethic, rooted in the law of Moses which instructed God's people to live together in love without hate, bitterness, or vengeance. It was new in that it would dominate and define how the followers of Jesus would answer every moral dilemma. The overarching question would now be, 'What is the loving thing to do?' This love ethic would be defined by Jesus' very death on the cross. Jesus said, 'Greater love has no one than this, that someone lay down his life for his friends' (John 15:13)."[6]

9. In serving the disciples, Jesus did not deny His power or authority (verse 3). He said that they called Him "Lord" and "Teacher" and rightly so (verse 13). What was Jesus teaching the disciples about leadership?

_____

_____

_____

_____

_____

_____

_____

_____

_____

_____

_____

_____

_____

_____

_____

_____

_____

_____

_____

_____

_____

_____

_____

_____

Your Response

In a sense, Jesus washes our feet too: as He cares for us in our weakness, sin, and wounds. British preacher Charles Spurgeon said,

> When Jesus Christ puts away from us day by day our daily infirmities and sins, does he not wash our feet? . . .
> The Lord Jesus loves his people so, that every day he is washing their feet. Their poorest action he accepts; their deepest sorrow he feels; their slenderest wish he hears, and their greatest sin he forgives. He is still their servant as well as their friend; still he takes the basin; still he wears the towel.[7]

Close your eyes and imagine Jesus washing your feet. Is there anything preventing you from allowing Jesus to wash your feet? How can you be in a posture of receiving this foot washing from Jesus?

For Further Study

Read Matthew 20:20-28. The mother of James and John knelt before Jesus to request that her sons receive favored positions in His Kingdom. Jesus listened to her request, but His reply was not what she expected. The path to "greatness" is a path of dying to self. To "drink the cup" that Jesus was going to drink meant taking up one's own cross to follow Him. How did Jesus use this opportunity to teach this mother and the other disciples what true servant leadership looks like? What did Jesus mean when He said, "whoever wants to become great among you must be your servant, and whoever wants to be first must be your slave" (verses 26-27)?

JESUS HOSTS THE LAST SUPPER

Luke 22:7-23

Maundy Thursday

[Jesus] took the cup, saying, "This
cup is the new covenant in my blood,
which is poured out for you."
LUKE 22:20

SINCE THE EXODUS, God's people had celebrated Passover, commemorating God's liberation of His people from Egypt. The Israelites had been enslaved and oppressed for centuries, and as part of His rescue, God told them to put the blood of a spotless lamb over their doorframes. The death of the firstborn sons had been the final warning to Pharaoh. The Passover lamb meant that the Israelites' firstborn sons would be spared from death (Exodus 12:1-14).

On this night, the final night before His crucifixion, Jesus expressed His longing to celebrate the Passover with His disciples. As He prepared His disciples for His death and resurrection, He gave the ancient symbols of the Passover new meaning. At this Passover, Jesus announced a new Passover Lamb: that through His sacrificial death as the Lamb of God, He would bring a new covenant for all people, ratified by His blood.

During His Last Supper, Jesus instituted what we now call Holy Communion, the Lord's Supper, or the Eucharist—not only for the twelve disciples but for all people and all generations to come. Whenever we eat the bread and drink the cup, we not only remember Jesus' death and resurrection but we also physically proclaim our trust in God's liberation of us by His body and blood. As New Testament scholar Scot McKnight writes,

> Jesus establishes for his followers a physical, sacred rhythm so they will never forget his gracious act of love for them. The bread and wine are his "tangible truth."[1]

While the Passover focused on the past, the Lord's Supper also looks to the present and future. We are spiritually strengthened by this physical act as we affirm Jesus' victory over sin, death, oppression, and injustice. And we look forward to Jesus' second coming, when He will restore all things and establish His Kingdom of righteousness forever.[2] Christ has died; Christ is risen; Christ will come again.

---

1. If you have taken Communion before, describe your experience. What is meaningful to you about eating the bread and drinking the cup? Is anything about Communion difficult for you?

_____

_____

_____

_____

_____

_____

_____

_____

_____

_____

_____

_____

_____

_____

2. Read Luke 22:7-23. What stands out to you?

_____

_____

_____

_____

_____

_____

_____

_____

_____

_____

3. Jesus knew His hour had come to suffer and die for us, so He enacted this Last Supper as a parting gift for the disciples and future generations. How was Jesus in control of all the events that transpired in this passage?

_____

_____

_____

_____

_____

_____

_____

_____

_____

_____

_____

_____

_____

_____

When John the Baptist saw Jesus, he identified Jesus as "the Lamb of God, who takes away the sin of the world!" (John 1:29).

The Greek term for "Passover" (*pascha*) is very close in spelling to the Greek term often used to speak of the "suffering" of Jesus (*paschō*). Many Jews and early Christians probably would have noticed and made a connection between the terms (see, for example, Luke 22:15).

4. How is Jesus' death a fulfillment of the Passover?

_____

_____

_____

_____

_____

_____

_____

_____

_____

_____

Both Jesus' resurrection and His final victory when He returns are joyful events. The early Christians in Acts understood this and celebrated Communion with "glad and generous hearts" (Acts 2:46, ESV).[3]

5. Jesus says He will not eat bread again "until it finds fulfillment in the kingdom of God" or drink wine again "until the kingdom of God comes" (verses 16 and 18). The Lord's Supper is both a meal of remembrance of Jesus' death and resurrection and an expectation of the fulfillment of the Kingdom of God. How does looking forward to the future reign of Jesus change the way we take Communion?

_____

_____

_____

_____

_____

_____

_____

_____

_____

_____

_____

_____

6. Jesus calls Himself the Bread of Life, who has come down from heaven to give life to the world (John 6:32-40). Reread Luke 22:19. What four verbs are used in connection with the bread? What is the significance of each?

_____

_____

_____

_____

_____

_____

_____

_____

_____

_____

7. In Matthew's Gospel, Jesus offers the cup of wine to the disciples, saying, "This is my blood of the covenant, which is poured out for many for the forgiveness of sins" (Matthew 26:28). How are we cleansed by the blood of Jesus?

_____

_____

_____

_____

_____

_____

_____

_____

_____

As our Great High Priest, Jesus entered the Most Holy Place, heaven itself, and paid for our sins once for all by His own blood. Old Testament priests sprinkled the blood of animals on those who were ceremonially unclean to make them outwardly clean (Hebrews 9:13). "How much more, then, will the blood of Christ, who through the eternal Spirit offered himself unblemished to God, cleanse our consciences from acts that lead to death," so that we are eternally redeemed to "serve the living God!" (Hebrews 9:14).

8. Read Jeremiah 31:31-34. How is the new covenant different from previous ones?

_____

_____

_____

_____

_____

_____

_____

_____

_____

9. Has this session enhanced your understanding of what it means to partake in Communion? If so, what have you learned, and how does that change your mindset and posture as you approach the table?

_____

_____

_____

_____

_____

_____

_____

_____

_____

_____

_____

_____

Your Response

If your tradition allows, take Communion with your family, friends, or those you are studying this session with. Remember how the early Christians in Acts ate together with "glad and generous hearts" (Acts 2:46, ESV). Serve one another the bread and the cup with joy and thanksgiving, repeating the words of Jesus from Luke 22:19-20.

For Further Study

Read Luke 24:30-35. After Jesus was crucified, two disciples were walking to Emmaus and discussing everything that had happened to Jesus. Jesus joined them on the journey and explained what the prophecies in Scripture said concerning Himself. Though their hearts were burning as Jesus spoke, the two disciples did not recognize Him. Once they reached Emmaus, Jesus sat down to break bread with them. Compare the verbs used in Luke 24:30 with the verbs used in Luke 22:19, describing the Last Supper. How did these two disciples finally come to recognize Jesus? Why is this significant?

_____

_____

_____

_____

_____

_____

_____

_____

_____

_____

_____

_____

_____

_____

_____

_____

_____

_____

_____

JESUS PRAYS AT GETHSEMANE

Matthew 26:36-46

Maundy Thursday

[Jesus prayed,] "My Father, if it is possible, may this cup be taken from me. Yet not as I will, but as you will."

MATTHEW 26:39

AFTER THE LAST SUPPER, Jesus took His disciples to pray at the garden of Gethsemane, located at the foot of the Mount of Olives.[1] Jesus knew the suffering that was coming. He was going to experience the betrayal of a disciple and denial by a close friend. People would give false testimony about Him, mock Him, and spit on Him. He would be flogged and ultimately die a painful death on a Roman cross. Though sinless, He was going to carry the full weight of the sins of the world on the cross. The worst part would be facing the abandonment and wrath of His Father while being punished for the sins of humanity.

No wonder Jesus told His friends that His soul was "overwhelmed with sorrow to the point of death" and asked them to keep watch for Him (Matthew 26:38). Jesus knew that when the soldiers came to arrest Him, His friends would abandon Him. Yet He shared His deepest emotions with Peter, James, and John.

Jesus then went a little farther alone, fell to the ground, and prayed, "My Father, if it is possible, may this cup be taken from me. Yet not as I will, but as you will" (Matthew 26:39). He returned to His friends three times, and each time they were asleep. Jesus' distress was so intense that His sweat became "like drops of blood falling to the ground" (Luke 22:44). Three times

He prayed these same agonizing words to His Father. How He longed for the cup to be removed! Ultimately, however, Jesus accepted that there was no other way and found strength to face the Cross.

---

1. Read Matthew 26:36-46. What stands out to you?

_____

_____

_____

_____

_____

_____

_____

_____

_____

2. Jesus was fully God and also fully human. How do you see His humanity displayed in this passage?

_____

_____

_____

_____

_____

_____

_____

_____

_____

_____

3. In His pain, Jesus didn't withdraw from God the Father, but rather fell prostrate on the ground, crying, "My Father" (Matthew 26:39). Mark's Gospel preserves the Aramaic: "Abba" (Mark 14:36). It can be difficult to approach God with honesty and vulnerability when we are in pain. How is Jesus' prayer a model for how to approach our Abba Father when we face hardship?

> Scot McKnight observes that Jesus chose to use the word *Abba* to address God, which evokes "God's unconditional, unlimited, and unwavering love for his people. In this name for God we are standing face-to-face with the very premise of spiritual formation: God loves us and we are his children."[2]

_____

_____

_____

_____

_____

_____

_____

4. When Jesus asks for the Father to remove the "cup," He may be alluding to God's cup of judgment. On the cross, the Father made the sinless Son to be sin for our sake (2 Corinthians 5:21) to save us from the wrath of God (Romans 5:9). Why do you think it was necessary for Jesus to not only suffer and die but also bear God's wrath?

> The cup was a common symbol for divine wrath in the Old Testament (Isaiah 51:17; Jeremiah 25:15-16; Ezekiel 23:33).

_____

_____

_____

_____

_____

_____

_____

_____

_____

_____

Tish Harrison Warren writes, "The work of Jesus continues, even now, in our everyday lives. So in hardship we do not look to Jesus solely as one who has been there before, once upon a time in a distant past. We find he is here with us, in the present tense. He participates in our suffering, even as—mysteriously—in our suffering we participate in the fullness of Christ's life."[3]

5. Have you ever prayed for God to remove a hardship . . . and the answer was no? Describe what that experience was like. How does it feel to know that Jesus also asked God for a way out and that He can empathize with what you are going through?

_____

_____

_____

_____

_____

_____

_____

_____

6. Ultimately, Jesus desired to do God's will and submitted Himself to it, knowing the full cost He would bear. He prayed, "Yet not as I will, but as you will" (Matthew 26:39) and "may your will be done" (verse 42). What do you think it took emotionally, physically, and spiritually for Jesus to pray this prayer?

_____

_____

_____

_____

_____

_____

_____

_____

_____

7. When Jesus saw that the disciples were asleep, He said, "The spirit is willing, but the flesh is weak" (Matthew 26:41). Jesus understood that His friends may have been spiritually eager to stay up and pray for Him, but they were physically vulnerable. How does Jesus' humanity give us confidence to come to Him in our times of need?

_____
_____
_____
_____
_____
_____
_____
_____

"Since then we have a great high priest who has passed through the heavens, Jesus, the Son of God, let us hold fast our confession. For we do not have a high priest who is unable to sympathize with our weaknesses, but one who in every respect has been tempted as we are, yet without sin. Let us then with confidence draw near to the throne of grace, that we may receive mercy and find grace to help in time of need" (Hebrews 4:14-16, ESV).

8. Jesus prays the same prayer three times. When Jesus finishes praying the third time, He appears composed and in complete control of the situation. He wakes up the disciples and tells them His hour has come, and the betrayer is coming. What do you think strengthened Jesus to face what was to come?

_____
_____
_____
_____
_____
_____
_____
_____
_____

In Luke's account, an angel from heaven appeared and strengthened Jesus (Luke 22:43).

9. Describe a time in your life when your circumstances may not have changed, but you felt strengthened to face your circumstances. How were you strengthened?

_____

_____

_____

_____

_____

_____

_____

_____

_____

_____

Christianity Today president and CEO Timothy Dalrymple writes, "Countless times throughout the history of the church, it has been the passionate love of the Christian that moves her to suffer with those who suffer from injustice or want and to bring hope and healing into places of pain.

"There is suffering in longing and longing in suffering, and sometimes it takes suffering to awaken or reawaken our desire for justice, community, and the final triumph of good."[4]

10. Jesus' willingness to submit to the agony of the Cross reveals the depth of God's love for us. Read John 3:16; Romans 5:6-8; and Ephesians 2:4-7. What can we learn from Jesus' model of suffering and love for us?

_____

_____

_____

_____

_____

_____

_____

_____

_____

Your Response

How do you pray when you're overwhelmed with disappointment, sorrow, or anger? Jesus' prayer shows that you can come to the Father in your hurting humanity. You do not have to wipe your tears or calm down before you kneel before the throne of God. Try bringing your raw emotion and desires to God. After you have expressed all that is in your heart to God, ask Him to help you release what you are holding into His loving hands. Jesus prayed the same prayer three times. It's okay if you don't have the "right" words or if all you can do is repeat the same words. If surrender is difficult, simply pray, *Help me pray, "Your will be done."*

For Further Study

Read the account of the Transfiguration in Luke 9:28-36. What similarities do you notice between the story of Jesus' glory in His transfiguration and His agony in Gethsemane? What do you think Moses and Elijah were talking to Jesus about? In what ways does the Transfiguration reveal Jesus' divinity?

_____

_____

_____

_____

_____

_____

_____

_____

_____

_____

_____

_____

_____

_____

_____

_____

_____

_____

_____

_____

_____

_____

JESUS' SEVEN LAST SAYINGS

Mark 15:33-41; Luke 23:32-46; John 19:25-30

Good Friday

Jesus said, "It is finished."

JOHN 19:30

FRIDAY IS THE DAY JESUS DIED. The events leading up to Jesus' death that day reveal how He was treated with extreme injustice and cruelty. Following Judas's betrayal and Jesus' arrest, He was taken to the high priest, who asked Him if He was the Messiah. "'I am,' said Jesus. 'And you will see the Son of Man sitting at the right hand of the Mighty One and coming on the clouds of heaven'" (Mark 14:62). At this, the high priest tore his clothes. The high priest and the Sanhedrin considered this blasphemy and worthy of death, but they did not have the power to execute Jesus. So they sent Him to Pontius Pilate, the Roman governor. Though Pilate could not find Jesus guilty of any charge, he yielded to political pressure from the Jewish leaders and crowd (Luke 23:13-23; John 19:12) and handed Jesus over for execution.

First, the Roman soldiers flogged and mocked Jesus. Then, with the help of Simon of Cyrene, Jesus carried a heavy wooden cross to a place outside the city called Golgotha (Mark 15:22). There Jesus was nailed to the cross next to two criminals. Darkness came over the whole land from noon to three. Even as Jesus suffered a brutal and humiliating death, His supreme love radiated through the last words He uttered.

In this final session, we will meditate on Jesus' seven declarations from the cross. We enter this last study somberly, considering the suffering Jesus endured because of His love for us. "There is no greater love than to lay down one's life for one's friends" (John 15:13, NLT). Some churches hold a Tenebrae service on Good Friday, extinguishing a candle after each reading until there is total darkness near the end of the service. You may decide to light seven candles before you begin this session and blow out a candle after you complete each question about His final words.

Author and Episcopal priest Fleming Rutledge writes, "There is nothing that you or I could ever do, or say, or be, that would put us beyond the reach of Jesus' prayers. Nothing at all. And ... no one else, no one at all, is beyond that reach. His prayer for the worst of the worst comes from a place beyond human understanding."[1]

1. **"Father, forgive them, for they do not know what they are doing."** Read Luke 23:32-34. Remarkably, the first words Jesus uttered from the cross were to pray for those who were crucifying Him. He interceded for those who shouted "crucify," who mocked Him, who falsely accused Him, and who nailed Him to the cross. What does Jesus' prayer reveal about His grace? How does this give you assurance that Jesus has fully forgiven you and invites you into an intimate relationship with God?

_____

_____

_____

_____

_____

_____

_____

_____

_____

_____

_____

_____

_____

2. **"Truly I tell you, today you will be with me in paradise."** Read Luke 23:39-43. Jesus was crucified next to two criminals who deserved to be punished for their crimes. How does Jesus' promise to the second criminal dismantle any notion that we can earn our salvation by good works? How does this give us hope for those in our lives who don't know Jesus? Spend a moment silently praying for someone you love who has not yet accepted Jesus as their Savior.

Jesus' response assures this criminal that he would enjoy an "immediate, joyful experience of fellowship with Jesus 'in paradise' (*en tō paradeisō*, GK 4137). This Persian word, which had been taken over into Greek, symbolizes a place of beauty and delight. It means 'park' or 'garden' and refers to the garden of Eden in Genesis 2:8 (LXX) and to the future bliss the garden symbolizes (Isa 51:3; cf. Rev 2:7)."[2]

_____

_____

_____

_____

_____

_____

_____

_____

_____

_____

_____

_____

_____

_____

_____

_____

_____

_____

_____

_____

_____

Unlike in our culture and language, the term *woman* here is used as a form of polite address.[3] On a micro-level, Jesus, even in the agony of the cross, is providing for the loneliness of His mother and the disciple He loved.[4] On a macro-level, Jesus was creating a new fellowship of the redeemed through His shed blood where the "bonds of Christian love surpass all natural barriers and bring into one great family all who love and follow Jesus."[5]

3. Jesus said to His mother, **"Woman, here is your son,"** and to the apostle John, **"Here is your mother."** Read John 19:25-27. Mary was probably a widow at this point and could not earn much income in that society. As the eldest son, Jesus was responsible for providing for her in her old age. Although Jesus had younger brothers, they may not have believed in Him yet (John 7:5). What do you think this adoption that Jesus performed from the cross demonstrates about the new kinds of relationships in His church?

_____

_____

_____

_____

_____

_____

_____

_____

_____

_____

_____

_____

_____

_____

_____

_____

_____

4. **"My God, my God, why have you forsaken me?"** Read Mark 15:33-41. Bearing the full weight of the sin of humanity, Jesus cried out in a loud voice: *"Eloi, Eloi, lema sabachthani?"* He had enjoyed intimate, unbroken communion with the Father for eternity, and now the Father had to turn His face away from Jesus. While we cannot comprehend the depth of Jesus' anguish, spend a few moments of silence contemplating the abandonment that Jesus must have felt. How can He empathize with us when we are in our deepest, darkest pain?

Jesus experienced God's cup of judgment, becoming a curse for us to redeem us from the curse of the law (Galatians 3:13-14). "God made him who had no sin to be sin for us, so that in him we might become the righteousness of God" (2 Corinthians 5:21).

"As the deer pants for streams of water, so my soul pants for you, my God. My soul thirsts for God, for the living God. When can I go and meet with God?" (Psalm 42:1-2). Author Philip Yancey writes that Mother Teresa made "I thirst" the motto of her order, the Sisters of Charity. For her, these words carry a deeper meaning than mere physical thirst: They also demonstrate God's thirst to draw humanity close to Himself. She wrote, "'We carry in our body and soul the love of an infinite thirsty God. . . . God thirsts for us and humanity thirsts for God.' God thirsts not out of need but out of desire, for God's essence is love."[6]

5. **"I am thirsty."** Read John 19:28-30. Few of us have experienced extreme thirst, but this detail shows Jesus' vulnerability and humanity. Jesus suffered immense thirst so He could quench our spiritual thirst forever and give us eternal life (John 4:14). What awakens us to our spiritual thirst? To what degree are you aware of your spiritual thirst? How is your thirst being satisfied?

_____

_____

_____

_____

_____

_____

_____

_____

_____

_____

_____

_____

_____

_____

_____

_____

_____

_____

_____

6. **"It is finished."** Read John 19:30. The statement "It is finished" is the translation of a single Greek word: *tetelestai*. This verb (from *teleō*) means "to bring to a close" in the sense of completion or fulfillment.[7] In John 4:34, Jesus told His disciples, "My food . . . is to do the will of him who sent me and to finish his work." Now it is finished. What does it mean to rest in the work Jesus accomplished on the cross while also continuing the work God has called you to do?

The verb form *tetelestai* is in the perfect tense in Greek. The perfect tense is typically used to express an action that has been completed in the past but whose results continue into the present. With this understanding, Jesus' cry "It is finished" connotes that it was finished in the past, it is still finished in the present, and it will remain finished in the future.[8]

_____

_____

_____

_____

_____

_____

_____

_____

_____

_____

_____

_____

_____

_____

_____

_____

_____

_____

_____

_____

_____

_____

_____

These last words of Jesus are a quote from Psalm 31:5, which was used by the Jews as an evening prayer.[9] Some liturgical Christian traditions include this prayer at Compline, the final prayer service of the day.[10]

7. **"Father, into your hands I commit my spirit."**
Read Luke 23:44-46. Jesus modeled how to live a life of love for others, and now He models how to sacrifice one's life for others. We can follow Jesus' example and commit our spirit into God's hands in whatever we face every day. Is there anything that you find difficult to commit into God's hands? What anxiety, decision, or hardship are you carrying right now? Take some time to pray and give each of these things to God. End the time of silence by praying aloud, "Father, into your hands I commit my spirit."

8. Pray and thank Jesus for choosing to endure all
   that He did for us on the cross, to be punished
   in our place, so that we could be healed by His
   wounds and have peace with God and others.
   Read Isaiah 53:1-12 aloud. Pause before you read
   verses 11-12. If you have candles, light the center
   candle and resume reading the remainder of the
   chapter. According to verses 11-12, what happened
   after Jesus suffered?

_____

_____

_____

_____

_____

_____

_____

_____

_____

_____

_____

_____

_____

_____

_____

_____

_____

_____

_____

_____

Your Response

Read Matthew 27:51-54. The veil that separated the Holy of Holies in the Temple was torn in two, symbolizing that because of Jesus' death, we now have direct access to God. When the Roman centurion and those guarding Jesus saw the earthquake and how Jesus died, they exclaimed, "Truly this was the Son of God!" (Matthew 27:54, ESV). As you reflect on this session and the other sessions in this study, what words, signs, or actions of Jesus stand out to you, pointing to how He truly is the Son of God? In what ways has Jesus revealed more of His love to you over the course of this study? If you have doubts or questions, ask Jesus to reveal Himself in those areas.

_____

_____

_____

_____

_____

_____

_____

_____

_____

_____

_____

_____

_____

_____

_____

_____

_____

_____

For Further Study

Read John 20:24-29. Thomas was not present when the risen Jesus first appeared to the disciples. Thomas declared that he would not believe unless he put his finger in the holes in Jesus' hands and his hand in Jesus' side. Thomas wanted to connect with Jesus not just by words and sight but by touching Jesus' crucifixion wounds. Just as Jesus welcomed Thomas to touch His wounds, we are invited also to an intimacy with Christ through sharing in His suffering (Philippians 3:10). What is the significance of Jesus eternally bearing the scars of His crucifixion? How do we participate in the sufferings of Christ? How does that shape us to be a source of comfort to others (2 Corinthians 1:3-5)?

EPILOGUE

THIS STUDY FOCUSED ON JESUS' LAST WEEK leading up to the Crucifixion, examining His love for us through the suffering and longing He experienced going to the Cross. People did not expect Jesus' Kingdom to be ushered in through His death. But on the cross, Jesus won the victory over sin and death, overthrew the powers of darkness, and opened the way for His coming Kingdom and for all people to know Him.

Yet Jesus' journey did not end there. On Saturday, Jesus descended into hell and brought salvation to the souls held captive there (Matthew 27:51-53; 1 Peter 3:18-19; 4:6). On Sunday, His tomb was found empty. Death was not the end. He rose again!

Jesus' resurrection marked the inauguration of the Kingdom of God, a new world order in which justice, salvation, and new creation have arrived at last.[1] After His resurrection, Jesus appeared to many of His followers, including Mary Magdalene and the other women at the tomb; the two disciples on the road to Emmaus; the eleven apostles; and five hundred brothers and sisters at the same time (1 Corinthians 15:6). In His appearances over the course of forty days, He spoke about the Kingdom of God and the coming of the Holy Spirit (Acts 1:3-5). Before Jesus ascended to heaven, He commissioned His followers:

> You will receive power when the Holy Spirit comes on you; and you will be my witnesses in Jerusalem, and in all Judea and Samaria, and to the ends of the earth.
> ACTS 1:8

As Jesus sent His first disciples, He is also sending us as His renewed people to bring His Kingdom on earth. Jesus told His followers that after He returned to the Father, they would do even greater things than He did (John 14:12). Equipped with the Holy Spirit, we participate as Kingdom bringers when we follow Jesus' footsteps: denying ourselves, taking up our crosses, and loving others as He loved us (Matthew 16:24; John 13:34-35). Let us pray that we can be a community of Kingdom bringers, living a life of worship and sacrificial love that is extended to the least of these.

May His Kingdom come on earth as it is in heaven. Amen.

NOTES

INTRODUCTION–JESUS' PASSION WEEK
1. Online Etymology Dictionary, s.v. "passion [n.]," accessed April 18, 2023, https://www.etymonline.com/word/passion.

SESSION 1–JESUS APPROACHES JERUSALEM
1. William Barclay, trans., *The Gospel of Luke* (Philadelphia: Westminster Press, 1956), 250.
2. Rome would besiege the city of Jerusalem and destroy the Temple in AD 70.
3. Walter L. Liefeld and David W. Pao, "Luke," in *The Expositor's Bible Commentary, Volume X*, rev. ed., eds. Tremper Longman III and David E. Garland (Grand Rapids, MI: Zondervan, 2007), 291–92.
4. Jason Porterfield, *Fight Like Jesus: How Jesus Waged Peace throughout Holy Week* (Harrisonburg, VA: Herald Press, 2022), 24.
5. Porterfield, *Fight Like Jesus*, 24–25.
6. Porterfield, *Fight Like Jesus*, 31–33.
7. Michael Chung, *The Last King of Israel: Lessons from Jesus's Final Ten Days* (Eugene, OR: Wipf & Stock, 2016), 44–45.
8. R. Alan Culpepper, "Luke," in *The New Interpreter's Bible Commentary, Volume IX: General Articles on the New Testament, the Gospel of Luke, the Gospel of John*, ed. Leander E. Keck (Nashville: Abingdon Press, 1995), 370.
9. Culpepper, "Luke," in *The New Interpreter's Bible Commentary, Volume IX*, 371.
10. N. T. Wright, *How God Became King: The Forgotten Story of the Gospels* (New York: Harper One, 2012), 264.
11. Wright, *How God Became King*, 246.
12. Wright, *How God Became King*, 118.
13. Blue Letter Bible, "Lexicon: Strong's G2799—*klaiò*," accessed April 18, 2023, https://www.blueletterbible.org/lexicon/g2799/niv/mgnt/0-1.
14. Tish Harrison Warren, *Prayer in the Night: For Those Who Work or Watch or Weep* (Downers Grove, IL: IVP, 2021), 51.

Notes

15. Mark Vroegop, *Dark Clouds, Deep Mercy: Discovering the Grace of Lament* (Wheaton, IL: Crossway, 2019), 26.
16. Porterfield, *Fight Like Jesus*, 37.

SESSION 2—JESUS CLEANSES THE TEMPLE

1. Craig S. Keener, *The IVP Bible Background Commentary: New Testament*, 2nd ed. (Downers Grove, IL: IVP Academic, 2014), 97.
2. Rich Villodas, *Good and Beautiful and Kind: Becoming Whole in a Fractured World* (Colorado Springs: WaterBrook, 2022), 189.
3. Jason Porterfield, *Fight Like Jesus: How Jesus Waged Peace throughout Holy Week* (Harrisonburg, VA: Herald Press, 2022), 59.
4. D. A. Carson, "Matthew," in *The Expositor's Bible Commentary, Volume IX: Matthew and Mark*, rev. ed., eds. Tremper Longman III and David E. Garland (Grand Rapids, MI: Zondervan, 2010), 499.
5. Carson, "Matthew" in *The Expositor's Bible Commentary, Volume IX*, 501–502.
6. Carson, "Matthew," in *The Expositor's Bible Commentary, Volume IX*, 502–503.
7. Alia Joy, *Glorious Weakness: Discovering God in All We Lack* (Grand Rapids, MI: Baker Books, 2019), 42.
8. N. T. Wright, *How God Became King: The Forgotten Story of the Gospels* (New York: Harper One, 2012), 247.

SESSION 3—JESUS TEACHES AT THE TEMPLE

1. Craig S. Keener, *The IVP Bible Background Commentary: New Testament*, 2nd ed. (Downers Grove, IL: IVP Academic, 2014), 159.
2. Morna D. Hooker, *The Gospel According to Saint Mark*, Black's New Testament Commentary (Peabody, MA: Hendrickson Publishers, 1991), 279.
3. Jason Porterfield, *Fight Like Jesus: How Jesus Waged Peace throughout Holy Week* (Harrisonburg, VA: Herald Press, 2022), 70.
4. Walter W. Wessel and Mark L. Strauss, "Mark," in *The Expositor's Bible Commentary, Volume IX*, rev. ed., eds. Tremper Longman III and David E. Garland (Grand Rapids, MI: Zondervan, 2010), 901.
5. Porterfield, *Fight Like Jesus*, 70.
6. Porterfield, *Fight Like Jesus*, 70.
7. Porterfield, *Fight Like Jesus*, 72. Porterfield is quoting Andreas Köstenberger and Justin Taylor, "The Escalating Conflict," in *Your Sorrow Will Turn to Joy: Morning and Evening Meditations for Holy Week* (Minneapolis, MN: Desiring God, 2016), 35.
8. N. T. Wright, *How God Became King: The Forgotten Story of the Gospels* (New York: Harper One, 2012), 150.
9. Porterfield, *Fight Like Jesus*, 74.

SESSION 4—JESUS IS ANOINTED AT BETHANY

1. Scholars disagree on which day the Bethany anointing took place since there are differences in the Gospel accounts. John appears to place this event upon Jesus' arrival in Bethany six days before the Passover. Mark places the dinner after the controversial Temple teachings that occurred on Tuesday and two days before the

Passover. Matthew also indicates that this meal occurred after the Temple teachings on Tuesday. This event isn't covered in Luke's Gospel.

2. Michael Chung, *The Last King of Israel: Lessons from Jesus's Final Ten Days* (Eugene, OR: Wipf & Stock, 2016), 66.
3. Jason Porterfield, *Fight Like Jesus: How Jesus Waged Peace throughout Holy Week* (Harrisonburg, VA: Herald Press, 2022), 114.
4. Bruce Manning Metzger, *The New Testament: Its Background, Growth, and Content* (Nashville, TN: Abingdon Press, 1965), 121.
5. Craig S. Keener, *The IVP Bible Background Commentary: New Testament*, 2nd ed. (Downers Grove, IL: IVP Academic, 2014), 285.
6. Keener, *The IVP Bible Background Commentary: New Testament*, 165.
7. Morna D. Hooker, *The Gospel According to Saint Mark*, Black's New Testament Commentary (Peabody, MA: Hendrickson Publishers, 1991), 329.
8. Blue Letter Bible, "Lexicon: Strong's G2570—*kalos*," accessed April 18, 2023, https://www.blueletterbible.org/lexicon/g2570/niv/mgnt/0-1.

SESSION 5—JESUS WASHES THE DISCIPLES' FEET
1. N. T. Wright, *How God Became King: The Forgotten Story of the Gospels* (New York: Harper One, 2012), 205.
2. Robert H. Mounce, "John," in *The Expositor's Bible Commentary, Volume X*, rev. ed., eds. Tremper Longman III and David E. Garland (Grand Rapids, MI: Zondervan, 2010), 545.
3. Mounce, "John," in *The Expositor's Bible Commentary, Volume X*, 547.
4. Mounce, "John," in *The Expositor's Bible Commentary, Volume X*, 546.
5. Gail R. O'Day, "John," in *The New Interpreter's Bible Commentary, Volume IX: General Articles on the New Testament, the Gospel of Luke, the Gospel of John*, ed. Leander E. Keck (Nashville: Abingdon Press, 1995), 727.
6. Derek Vreeland, "A Bright Shining Light: Five Things Revealed to Us by John's Jesus," N.T. Wright Online, accessed March 24, 2023, https://www.ntwrightonline.org/a-bright-shining-light-five-things-revealed-to-us-by-johns-jesus.
7. Charles Haddon Spurgeon, "Jesus Washing His Disciples' Feet," The Spurgeon Center, January 29, 1865, Metropolitan Tabernacle Pulpit Volume 11, https://www.spurgeon.org/resource-library/sermons/jesus-washing-his-disciples-feet/#flipbook.

SESSION 6—JESUS HOSTS THE LAST SUPPER
1. Scot McKnight, *The Jesus Creed: Loving God, Loving Others* (Brewster, MA: Paraclete Press, 2009), 270.
2. Justo L. González, *The Story Luke Tells: Luke's Unique Witness to the Gospel* (Grand Rapids, MI: Eerdmans, 2015), 109.
3. González, *The Story Luke Tells*, 106.

SESSION 7—JESUS PRAYS AT GETHSEMANE
1. Gethsemane literally means "oil press," the place where oil is squeezed from olives. D. A. Carson, "Matthew," in *The Expositor's Bible Commentary, Volume IX: Matthew and Mark*, rev. ed., eds. Tremper Longman III and David E. Garland (Grand Rapids, MI: Zondervan, 2010), 608.

2. Scot McKnight, *The Jesus Creed: Loving God, Loving Others* (Brewster, MA: Paraclete Press, 2009), 25.

3. Tish Harrison Warren, *Prayer in the Night: For Those Who Work or Watch or Weep* (Downers Grove, IL: IVP, 2021), 30.

4. Timothy Dalrymple, "What Passion Week Means," *Christianity Today*, April 6, 2020, https://www.christianitytoday.com/ct/2020/april-web-only/what-passion-week -means.html.

SESSION 8—JESUS' SEVEN LAST SAYINGS

1. Fleming Rutledge, *The Seven Last Words from the Cross* (Grand Rapids, MI: Eerdmans, 2005), 11.

2. Walter L. Liefeld and David W. Pao, "Luke," in *The Expositor's Bible Commentary, Volume X*, rev. ed. ed. Tremper Longman III and David E. Garland (Grand Rapids, MI: Zondervan, 2010), 334.

3. Robert H. Mounce, "John," in *The Expositor's Bible Commentary, Volume X*, rev. ed., eds. Tremper Longman III and David E. Garland (Grand Rapids, MI: Zondervan, 2010), 635.

4. William Barclay, trans., *The Gospel of John, Volume 2* (Philadelphia: Westminster Press, 1956), 299.

5. Mounce, "John," in *The Expositor's Bible Commentary, Volume X*, 636.

6. Mother Teresa, as quoted in Philip Yancey, *Vanishing Grace: Bringing Good News to a Deeply Divided World* (Grand Rapids, MI: Zondervan, 2018), 104.

7. Blue Letter Bible, "Lexicon: Strong's G5055—*teleò*," accessed April 18, 2023, https://www.blueletterbible.org/lexicon/g5055/niv/mgnt/0-1.

8. Blue Letter Bible, "Lexical Definitions—Perfect Tense," accessed April 18, 2023, https://www.blueletterbible.org/help/lexicalDefinitions.cfm?lang=G&num=5778.

9. Eli Lizorkin-Eyzenberg, "Rethinking Jesus' Words from the Hebrew Original," Israel Bible Weekly, April 2, 2023, https://weekly.israelbiblecenter.com/rethinking-jesus -words-hebrew-original.

10. "An Order for Compline," Book of Common Prayer online, accessed March 28, 2023, https://www.bcponline.org/DailyOffice/compline.html, 129.

EPILOGUE

1. N. T. Wright, *How God Became King: The Forgotten Story of the Gospels* (New York: Harper One, 2012), 269.

LifeChange

A NAVPRESS BIBLE STUDY SERIES

LifeChange Bible studies train you in good Bible study practices even as you enjoy a robust and engaging Bible study experience. Learn the skill as you study the Word. There is a study for every book of the Bible and relevant topics.

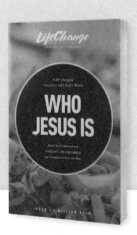

MAKE DISCIPLESHIP
A LIFESTYLE

THE 2:7 SERIES
Discipleship training with a proven track record

DESIGN FOR DISCIPLESHIP
Over 7 million sold

THE WAYS OF THE ALONGSIDER
For small groups, classes, or one-on-one discipling